Surviving the Sift

Surviving the Sift

Otescia R. Johnson

B.O.Y.
ENTERPRISES
Always Bet On Yourself

Lowell, NC

SURVIVING THE SIFT.

Please direct all copyright inquiries to:

B.O.Y. Publications, Inc.
c/o Author Copyrights
P.O. Box 262
Lowell, NC 28098
betonyourselfent.com

Paperback ISBN: 978-1-955605-37-3
eBook ISBN: 978-1-955605-40-3

Cover and Interior Design: B.O.Y. Enterprises, Inc.

Printed in the United States.

Dedication

To my spiritual parents, Pastors Eddie and Val Scarbrough, whose labor of love in the Kingdom raised this daughter to levels she never imagined.

TABLE OF CONTENTS

Introduction

Have you ever experienced a season of life that made you want to just run away from everything and everyone? No matter how hard you prayed, it felt like you just kept getting hit by one thing after another. You tried fasting, but the attacks just kept coming. You tried listening to your favorite preachers, but it didn't break. You tried crying out to God in prayer and felt comfort while praying, but as soon as you came out of prayer, more bad news was waiting to greet you. Sound familiar?

Many people like to say they feel like the enemy threw everything except the kitchen sink at them. I say the opposite. When I was experiencing my season of hardship, he threw everything INCLUD-ING the kitchen sink, which is why you'll see me refer to these intense seasons of war-fare as "kitchen sink" attacks. The most re-cent attack I experienced was so brutal, so unrelenting, that I toyed with the idea of running away. And I don't mean this figura-tively. I, a full-grown 40 plus year old woman, literally contemplated running away.

To give you a little glimpse into my personal life, my husband and I are the proud parents of 9 adult children, our blended crew of six, plus 3 wonderful chil-dren-in-love. We have the extreme joy of seven grandchildren, who remind us daily that having grandchildren is much more fun than having children. Plus, we have the added responsibility of being caregivers for my parents, who are both living with physi-cal and mental differences. Adding to our family dynamic are our responsibilities to serve in our local church, working full-time, and running a full-time business. To say our life is full would be an understatement. However, we love our family dearly; we thank God for our ever-growing crew daily, and we are grateful to be chosen to love and lead them.

Now, with that being said, being thankful for our family does not mean there aren't moments when the weight of the assignment feels too heavy. During our most recent "kitchen sink" attack, we felt as though we were being hit with blow after blow of hardship. I sat in the passenger seat of our car as my husband drove down the interstate and cried. As the tears silently rolled down my face, the following thoughts crossed my mind.

You know, you two have raised your children. They are adults. No one would blame you if you left them to figure out life on their own. You did your part.

Otescia R. Johnson

You've been taking care of your parents for over a decade, and you have served them well. No one would blame you for finding a nursing home for them. You deserve a break, especially after all this.

You guys wouldn't be under this financial pressure if you weren't taking care of everyone else.

You guys can go back to the west coast and start over, just the two of you. Your friends would allow you to stay in their basement while you find jobs and figure out your next move.

You're human. You can only take so much. Everyone has a breaking point. Be kind to yourself. Just go and start over without any guilt.

You've been taking care of other people for 26 years. When will you really take care of you?

Those heart palpitations you feel are stress. Remember what the doctor said in 2017. This stress will kill you.

As these thoughts raced through my mind, I welcomed them and mentally agreed with them. I have been taking care of other people most of my life. My children are adults who have what they need to excel in life. I have taken care of my parents and ensured they have a place to live since 2013. I put my dreams on hold to ensure my mother recovered from a serious illness. My husband and I have worked our fingers to the bone to provide for everyone financially. I agreed with the thoughts because every thought being thrown at me was rooted in facts. I couldn't think of a reason to disagree until a seemingly small thought occurred to me.

What about church? I can't abandon my church during this transition we're in.

Then another thought was thrown at me. *You don't owe them anything. You've served well while you were there, but now it's time for you and your husband to focus on what you need to recover. After the battle you've been in, you deserve a break. You deserve time to just be. No one can blame you for taking the time to catch your breath.*

I must be honest. The sound of a break and rest from the intense onslaught of attacks felt amazing. I allowed myself, just for a moment, to imagine what it would be like if it were just my husband and me in a new city where no one really knew us. We'd have an opportunity to just focus on ourselves and how we want to prepare for retirement. The more I thought about it, the more attractive it sounded. In fact, it was so attractive; it was seductive. And that's when it hit me… or I should say, that's when Holy Spirit revealed it to me. I'd been having a conversation with the devil, not myself.

The idea of running away felt so seductive because the enemy was literally attempting to seduce me into abandoning my post. He wanted me to walk away from my responsibilities to my parents, children, grandchildren, business clients, and my church family. He tempted me with rest because he knew he'd been pressuring me and my husband for months and I was mentally hanging on by a thread. And he almost had me, but thank God, 1 Corinthians 10:13 became spirit life to me when I needed it the most.

"We all experience times of testing, which is normal for every human being. But God will be faithful to you, He will screen and filter the severity, nature, and timing of every test or trial you face so that you can bear it. And each test is an opportunity to trust him more, for along with every trial God has provided for you a way of escape that will bring you out of it victoriously." **1 Corinthians 10:13 (TPT)**

That moment in the car became the starting point for the turning of the tide. Once Holy Spirit revealed I was being seduced in hopes, I'd throw in the towel, I sought the Lord for instructions on how to withstand the onslaught and walk in the victory promised to me in His word.

"Now thanks be to God, who always leads us in triumph in Christ, and through us diffuses the fragrance of His knowledge in every place." **– 2 Corinthians 2:14 (NKJV)**

Armed with the assurance of victory, the next 4 weeks became a testament of the faithfulness of God. As my family and I went from back-to-back attacks to back-to-back blessings and open doors; we literally watched God perform His word! As I journaled to keep a record of God's goodness, I heard the phrase, "Surviving the Sift". I wasn't sure what it meant, so I wrote it down and went on about my day. Day after day, I heard the same phrase until God spoke to my heart concerning the urgency of this message.

Surviving the Sift

Throughout the pages of this book, you'll discover insights into the challenges you've encountered, effective strategies for combat, and the essential tools you need to withstand the brutal assaults the enemy thought would make you curse God and die. You will learn how to not only survive the attack but how to live in your God-given dominion and experience the Supernatural move of God in the heat of the battle.

This is the seventeenth book I have written, and it is without a shadow of doubt the most crucial for the Body of Christ. May your faith be increased as you read and digest God's word to His body. Let all who have an ear hear what the Spirit is saying to the Church.

Chapter 1

What does "sift as wheat" mean?

"Peter, my dear friend, listen to what I'm about to tell you. Satan has obtained permission to come and sift you all like wheat and test your faith." **-Luke 22:31 (TPT)**

I f you are anything like me, the phrase, "sift you all like wheat" sounds utterly confusing. To understand this phrase, one must examine the process of sifting wheat as they handled it in Biblical days. Let's break down this process.

Step One: Threshing

The first step of the sifting process is threshing. During this step, the chaff is loosened from the edible grain. The old-fashioned way of doing this is to spread the wheat onto a floor made from stone, concrete, or tamped earth, and to beat it repeatedly with a flail.

A flail is an agricultural instrument made from two sticks tied together by a piece of leather. The farmer would hold one stick and use it to swing the other stick to strike the wheat. During the threshing process, the chaff, the hard outer shell, is forcibly separated from the valuable parts of the harvest.

One definition of chaff is worthless or trash. While the chaff is considered worthless after they have harvested the wheat, it actually helps to protect the grain while it is maturing. The hard outer shell is indigestible for humans. Therefore, once the grain has matured, what protected it in its former season must be removed before

Otescia R. Johnson

they can process the grain into whatever its final form will become.

Remember when we discussed feeling like you were being hit with blow after blow? This is literally the first step in the sifting process. While the enemy believes this process will cause you to lose hope and faint in the heat of the battle, what's actually happening is God is separating the dead, useless things from you. Even though those things may have served you well in the past, God knows your future and understands those things are no longer needed. He is intentionally and forcibly removing the things that can no longer serve you as you mature into the man or woman God always destined you to become.

Satan believes the "sifting" will be the end of the thing, but God KNOWS the sifting is just the beginning. Threshing is painful, but it is also beneficial. And no matter how long you've been saved, you will experience threshing repeatedly as you mature in Christ. Why? Because at every new level, a shedding of your hard exterior shell is required. The things that allowed you to self-protect and self-promote in your last season will not be permitted in your new season, hence, a new round of threshing comes before every major promotion in your life.

Step 2: Winnowing

In the second step of the sifting process, they remove the loosened chaff from the grain. In Biblical times, the grain and chaff were both thrown into the air. The lighter, useless chaff is easily blown away by the breeze. The heavier, valuable grain falls back to the ground. This process is repeated until all that remains is the weighty grain.

If threshing is when you feel like blow after blow is hitting you so fast and hard you can barely catch your breath; winnowing is when you feel people and things are constantly leaving you or being taken away from you. This process is painful because it can make you feel as though you are losing everything.

In your winnowing process, you may cry out to God, "How am I supposed to do what you've called me to do without the tools I need to do it? How can I build without people to help me build it?" During winnowing, the enemy wants to make you feel as though all signs are pointing towards you, closing your business or church. He'll tell you things like, this is no longer profitable, or he'll suggest your church is dying. He may even tell you the season for this thing is over and use the amount of people who have walked out of the door as his evidence.

Here's the thing though; you have a promise written in the book of Philippians.

"And my God shall supply all your need according to His riches in glory by Christ Jesus." **– Philippians 4:19 (NKJV)**

Although winnowing feels as though the things being removed from you are things you need, God knows you no longer need them. He has promised to provide all you need. Therefore, any person or thing that is removed from your life is someone or something you no longer need. That person or thing served you for the season, they/it was intended to serve you. Now, as God preps you for promotion and advancement, those things MUST be removed. They are now considered as "trash" to your life. Of course, the person or thing isn't trash, nor has their value diminished.

Yet, as it pertains to their place in your life, they are no longer needful.

When we see the things that have been removed from us through this lens of "winnowing," we stop longing for yesterday's provision and hold fast to the truth of God's daily bread. **What** you need today is what is here today. **Who** you need today is who is here today! The Devil would love to trick you into a place of mourning and depression over all you've lost, but I submit this is a moment to rejoice.

Winnowing is the last step of the sifting process. After chaff is removed, all that's left is what is valuable. This is why we rejoice. Because at the end of this process, we'll be in position to walk into the greatest season of our lives. Whether you walk into this season with 200 people at your side, or 2 people at your side, you have what you need because you LIVE in God's promise of provision. Whether you have 6 or 7 figures in your bank account or if your bank account is in the negative, you have what you need because you LIVE in the promise of provision!

Satan will try to make you feel as though you are losing things because of something you have done. He will tell you your sin, your obstinance, your ambition, your mismanagement, or your inability to plan for lean times is the reason you are experiencing this great falling away of people and things. This is a lie! He is the father of lies who is incapable of telling the truth. Sifting has nothing to do with your sins or anything else you may have done wrong. Sifting is a mandatory process that MUST happen prior to God's promotion.

Your faith MUST be tested. The hard outer shell that caused you to believe you could provide for or protect yourself MUST be removed. Your reliance on people who served you in former seasons MUST be removed. Your dependence on your savings account MUST be removed. Your adherences to worldly systems and patterns of belief MUST be removed. No matter how "saved" you are or how long you've walked with God, the process of sifting will be a reoccurrence. It doesn't mean you failed the last time. It simply means you are ready for the next level.

Sifting is the Final Exam

If we compare sifting to traditional education, sifting would be the final exam. It is the culmination of all they have taught you in the class and a test to see how much of the content you have mastered. The area you are being sifted in is directly related to what God needed you to learn before you're promoted.

With that in mind, if the time of sifting is related to your money, meaning you've experienced a drastic decrease in income or a time of back-to-back unexpected expenses, God is actually preparing to promote you in the area of your money. If the time of sifting is related to your ministry, meaning invitations to preach may have dried up or people may be walking out of your church by the dozens, God is preparing to promote you in the area of ministry. If the time of sifting is related to your health, meaning you've experienced a negative diagnosis or multiple illnesses back-to-back, God is preparing you for a physical promotion. He is prepping you to walk in the physical manifestation of His healing. The enemy thinks he is about to rob you of life, but God knows He is simply testing you to ensure you are ready to become His walking billboard for healing!

> **You are experiencing this sifting because God chose you as His vessel before the foundations of the world.**

Remember, everything God does or allows has purpose attached to it. You are not going through this simply because the enemy randomly picked you to pick on. You are experiencing this sifting because God chose you as His vessel before the foundations of the world. This purpose was placed in you before you were assigned to your mother's womb.

If Christians would truly grasp that God does EVERYTHING for our good, we'd understand this hell that was unleashed wasn't allowed to break us down, it was allowed to break every empty thing off us so all that is left is the SUBSTANCE God sent to the EARTH for HIS purpose.

Satan requests to "sift" us because he thinks it will remove us from our faith. God permits sifting because He knows it separates us from all the inconsequential parts that MUST be removed BEFORE He promotes, rewards, and elevates us! When you survive the sift, you essentially prove to God you are ready to be promoted. The old things that kept your heart hard towards Him have now been beaten off you and blown away! Now you are ready to walk into the greatest season you've ever experienced. You've been battle tested and proven ready for the next level. Rejoice!

Chapter 2

A Way of Escape

Have you ever seen or heard of someone throwing spaghetti at a wall to see if it sticks? The idea is totally gross to me, but it is said that if the spaghetti sticks to the wall, that means it's done. As you walk through the sifting process, you will be tempted by many thoughts. I like to think of it as the devil's version of throwing spaghetti at the wall. He throws thoughts at you, attempting to break you down mentally. The thoughts that "stick" are the ones that take your focus off God and what He is doing in and through you.

In the example I gave of me riding in the car thinking all those crazy thoughts, the enemy was throwing spaghetti and my mind was the wall. The thoughts were sticking because, as I stated, they were rooted in natural facts. Notice, I didn't say they were true, but when I took my eyes off God and started looking at things in the natural realm, I saw and received the facts of those thoughts. Those facts were depressing and led to me staring out the window and crying.

But remember, Holy Spirit also spoke to me. He gave me a single thought! While the enemy threw multiple thoughts at me to take my attention and focus off God, it only took one thought from Holy Spirit to bring me back to myself and the TRUTH.

"We all experience times of testing, which is normal for every human being. But God will be faithful to you. He will screen and filter the

severity, nature, and timing of every test or trial you face so that you can bear it. And each test is an opportunity to trust Him more, for along with every trial God has provided for you a way of escape that will bring you out of it victoriously. **– 1 Corinthians 10:13 (TPT)**

The most important element you will need to manage during sifting is your mind. What you think leads to feelings. Feelings lead to actions. This means thinking on the wrong things during a time of sifting can result in actions that hinder your success in this process. The devil is always going to attack you in your thought process, but even more so when your promotion is at hand. He's going to exploit every insecurity and fear you have NOT surrendered to God. But remember, God always provides a way of escape for you.

This season of sifting was only allowed because God knew you could handle it. In 1 Corinthians 10:13, we have a promise that God will screen and filter the severity, nature and timing of every test and trial you face SO THAT YOU CAN BEAR IT! You are guaranteed victory because God does not allow the enemy to throw things at you that you cannot handle. Remember, the devil has to get permission to sift you. This means God could have and would have said no if the enemy was going to throw something at you that you couldn't handle. Therefore, during a time of sifting, your confession must be, "if it's here, I can handle it!"

Your adversary would love to make you feel as though this is too much for you. And the truth is, most of us agree with him when we say things like, "this is too much" or "God, I can't take this anymore." When you release those words out of your mouth, not only are you signaling to the enemy that his spaghetti is sticking to the walls of your mind, but you are also giving him permission to continue throwing it. You are defeating yourself with your own words. What you speak shapes your world. So, if you confess failure, you will see failure even though you have a promise of victory!

God will never put you in a situation or allow the enemy to concoct a situation without a plan of escape for you. Even in the darkest of times, during the seemingly impossible moments, God has already seen the end from the beginning and made a way of escape for you. Your responsibility during the time of sifting is to feed yourself with the Word of God so that your tongue is always armed with the two-edged sword.

> **"...Each test is an opportunity to trust Him more..."**

When you view your sifting as an opportunity to trust God, you position yourself for a miracle. No longer will you view yourself as a victim who is being targeted. This shift in perspective is simple but powerful! It empowers you to see God trusted you enough to allow Satan to sift you because He knew you could handle it. God invited you to trust Him so He could perform His word and keep His promises to you.

You Have Fire Insurance

When you buy a house, you are required to purchase homeowner's insurance. This insurance ensures your home is protected from a myriad of things, so in the event a disaster should strike, the insurance company would cover the expenses to restore the home.

A close friend of mine experienced a flameless fire. This means the home was enveloped in damaging smoke, but there were no flames, so the structure of the home remained intact. Her homeowner's insurance stepped in to repair the damages to the home, but the area they focused the most attention on was the kitchen because that is where the most damage was done. Now, my friend is a lover of all things beautiful. When she and her husband purchased their home, it was an older, pre-existing home that needed a few updates. There were things about the home she did not find beautiful, but she knew they could make it beautiful together.

When the fire happened, and the insurance company began the process of restoring what was lost, this gave my friend the opportunity to beautify the kitchen she already wanted to upgrade. Of course, no family wants to be displaced from their home or experience a fire, but the opportunity to have the home restored with modern fixtures, appliances, cabinets, and flooring was a blessing in disguise. My friend and her husband could have allowed the devil to make them feel terrible about their situation, but together they survived the sift by seeing the way of escape God made for them. They restored the home without having to spend tens of thousands of dollars because the insurance company took care of the majority of the bill.

This is what happens when you experience a sifting. The enemy feels like he is turning the fire up in your life to punish you until you curse God. However, God is inviting you to pull on your fire insurance in Heaven. He is inviting you to allow Heaven to do the heavy lifting during this process. You've prayed for upgrades in your finances, relationships, health, career, business, home, or ministry. Those upgrades come by way of sifting. And on the other side of your sifting, you don't get returned to your original condition. You get the upgrades and modern advances you've wanted but couldn't afford on your own. God always restores BETTER than the original condition. Your job is only to trust Him and use the way of escape He provides.

Make no mistake, the way you see your sifting directly correlates to your end result. If you see this as an insurmountable test, you'll walk away from your assured victory. If you see this as an opportunity to trust God and watch Him flex on your behalf, you'll witness the greatest move and manifestation of the promises of God you've ever seen. Every season of sifting will push you into higher and higher levels of God's glory. Each time, you'll look back and see how far you've come. You'll witness first-hand the power of trusting and depending on the God who already made a way of escape for you!

"The eyes of the Lord search the whole earth in order to strengthen those whose hearts are fully committed to him..." **– 2 Chronicles 16:9 (NLT)**

Chapter 3

Eyes to See

"If people can't see what God is doing, they stumble all over themselves; But when they attend to what he reveals, they are most blessed." **– Proverbs 29:18 MSG**

Have you ever wondered if God knew what He was doing? It's okay, we can be honest in this book. Have you looked at a situation in your life and thought, there is no possible way this can work out? Most of us, if we're being truthful, would answer yes to both questions. In theory, we know God does not make mistakes, but when it looks like all the doors have closed in our face and trouble is coming from every corner, it is human nature to want to "see" a way out of your situation.

I am a full-time writer, publisher, and entrepreneur. I have a profitable company, but in the early years there were many tears shed because I knew God told me to walk away from traditional employment, but I could not *see* how my family would have the finances we needed. That lack of sight, not being able to see or discern God's plan, caused me to stumble through my journey of entrepreneurship.

Just as we discussed, God's promised way of escape in the last chapter, we also have a promise of vision. However, like all promises in the Bible, we must be in the proper position to receive it. In the example of entrepreneurship, God revealed to me I was called to become a business owner and working full-time for someone else was not His plan for me. It was then my responsibility to attend to what He revealed.

Initially, I did not have wisdom in this area, so instead of attending to what was revealed, I prayed, cried, and begged God to say something different. I fasted and prayed for a door of employment to be opened for me. When the door was not opened, I wallowed in self-pity and frustration. I was experiencing a "sift" in business and had no clue what was happening or how to survive it. God, in His infinite wisdom and faithfulness, sent my spiritual mother to bring correction and reveal what I was battling.

"Never let the enemy move you out of your place of provision because of frustration. You need to pray for God to

send you the right clients and the right team to help you.”

Although I still thought I wanted out when she spoke these words to me, this was the beginning of God opening my eyes to see what He was doing. I began to pray for God to help me see my life and business from His perspective. I spent time repeating what God released to me in prayer and through those I trusted. I leaned into His promises of provision and let go of my desire to do things my way. In other words, I began to “attend to what He revealed.” As I yielded my plan in favor of God’s plan for me, the frustration lifted.

God revealed to me how the devil was sifting me away from the business I was ordained to run by making me feel frustrated and overwhelmed. I felt as though I’d done all I could to grow the business and would not see the success I desired in that line of work. Just like the devil lied to me in the car, he lied to me about my business, and I believed Him.

When I meditated on the words my spiritual mother released to me and asked God to expound on them, I realized the exact moment the devil got to me. God revealed the devil's plan and devices so I could defeat them through His Word! Now that the enemy had been found out, he owed me seven times what I lost during the year I stumbled all over myself. His lies caused me to stumble, therefore he'd stolen from me, and I was determined to recover everything I lost.

"Excuses might be found for a thief who steals because he is starving. But if he is caught, he must pay back seven times what he stole, even if he has

to sell everything in his house." **– Proverbs 6:30-31 (NLT)**

The plans and weapons of the enemy are revealed so we can take authority over them through the Word of God and the power that lies within our tongue. God gives us eyes to see so we do not walk away from the promotion that comes after we survive the sift. Remember, God would not have given the enemy permission to sift you if He had not already prepared you to win. It's a fixed fight! Your responsibility is to pray for eyes to see what is being thrown at you AND God's strategy for your victory.

A Biblical example of when the enemy tried to frustrate someone into walking away from their promise happened when Laban tricked Jacob into marrying Leah, then attempted to steal the animals Jacob needed to leave Laban's home. You can find this story in Genesis 29:13-27 & Genesis 30:25-43.

Laban promised to give Rachel to Jacob after 7 years of work, but tricked Jacob and gave Leah to him instead. Then, when Jacob confronted Laban, the dishonest man only agreed to keep his original agreement if Jacob agreed to work another seven years. Can you imagine how frustrated you would be if you kept your end of a business deal and the person changed their mind and said, you can't have what we originally agreed to unless you double the time you work for me? Jacob could have become frustrated and walked away with Leah, but if he had, he would have missed his opportunity to marry Rachel and the opportunity to become wealthy. There would be no Joseph to rise to prominence in Egypt and provide restoration and safety to his family if Jacob would have allowed frustration to sift him!

> Time is one of the major ways the devil attempts to sift us.

The enemy tries to frustrate us with the amount of time we have been waiting to see a promise come to fruition. He tells us things like, "After all these years you should be further along than you are," or, "You've been serving God for 20 years and you're still living paycheck to paycheck." The frustration with time is a major weapon in the enemy's arsenal. This is why we must pray for God to give us eyes to see what is being used against us.

Instead of walking away, Jacob gave us an excellent example of how to trust God's appointed time to be revealed. And in doing so, when Jacob left Laban, Jacob was far wealthier than his former employer. What should have been a source of frustration in the natural became an opportunity for God to keep His promise to Jacob's grandfather Abraham. When you see what the enemy is doing, you can also see what God is doing. God was allowing the enemy to test Jacob because God knew Jacob would find wealth by mating the animals with the strategy God gave him. Jacob's responsibility was to keep his eyes on what God was doing so he could withstand the test of time.

The Test of Time

In Luke 22:31 TPT, Jesus revealed to Peter that Satan had obtained permission to sift them like wheat AND test their faith. As I mentioned earlier, one way the enemy attempts to test you is by delaying the thing

God has promised. Demonic delay is often an effective tactic during the sifting process, because most people have not developed the patience to endure until they see what God has promised.

It's important to note the sifting process is rarely swift. If the enemy knows you have no problem enduring for six months, he's not going to really turn up the fire until you get close to the sixth month because he believes that is your breaking point. Like God, the devil exits outside of time, so whether it takes six months or six years to get you to throw in the towel does not matter to him. He only cares about sifting until you break. He's persistent and crafty. He gets satisfaction when you cry about how long you've been waiting because he knows your tears of exhaustion mean you have not opened your eyes to see YOU control time!

Otescia R. Johnson

In the tenth chapter of Joshua, during an intense time of warfare, Joshua **prayed** to the Lord, but **spoke** to the sun and the moon. *"Then Joshua spoke to the Lord in the day when the Lord delivered up the Amorites before the children of Israel, and he said in the sight of Israel: Sun, stand still over Gibeon; And Moon, in the Valley of Aijalon."* – **Joshua 10:12 (NKJV).** While Joshua was praying to God, he was also using his authority to take dominion over the Earth. And because the Earth does not have free will, it was forced to go against its typical laws of nature to do exactly what Joshua commanded.

"So the sun stood still, And the moon stopped, till the people had revenge upon their enemies."
-Joshua 10:13 (NKJV)

Joshua understood the Lord was on his side and had given him a promise of victory. Yet, time was making it appear as

51

though he would not be able to finish the battle. Instead of crumbling or doubting the Lord's promise of victory, Joshua commanded time. Whether it appears time is being delayed or time is moving too fast, time is a created thing and once you use your God-given authority to give time a directive, it must obey!

There is no need to allow the enemy to tempt you into depression when time seems to be delayed. Instead, command the Earth to yield her increase to you today! (Psalm 67:6). Instead of allowing the enemy to make you frazzled about how little time you have to meet a deadline or complete a task, issue a declaration over your life and mind.

I decree and declare I have enough time to accomplish all I need to accomplish. I was graced for this assignment, and I will not allow time, a created thing, to make me feel anxious, frazzled, or frustrated!

Do you see the power you have when your eyes are opened to the plots, plans, tricks, and entrapments of the enemy? God is revealing all of this to you, so you will remain steadfast during the test of time. Think of it this way: does it really matter how long you take to achieve a thing once that thing has been achieved? For most of us, we forget how long we waited the second we see the manifestation.

If you are a person who does not mind waiting or if you have built up endurance in the area of your faith, your season of sifting may be much longer than the person who is new in their walk with Christ. Since you can withstand more, the enemy will keep throwing things at you for years before you finally get to the "kitchen sink attack". This means he'll save his most severe attack until the moment he thinks you've become weak. Do not be fooled by this tactic. His plot has been revealed. Your eyes are now opened to his devices. Now, your job is to withstand the test of time.

A prayer to see…

"And the Lord said to Joshua: 'See! I have given Jericho into your hand, its king, and the mighty men of valor.'"

—Joshua 6:2 (NKJV)

Father, in the name of Jesus, I pray now that you will open my eyes to see just as you commanded Joshua to see. Allow me to see the plots and plans of the enemy, so I will no longer be tricked into frustration, distraction, depression, and/or disappointment. I receive your commandment to SEE that You issued to Joshua. Thank you for allowing me to see what YOU are doing, so I will no longer stumble over myself, instead I will attend to what YOU reveal in Jesus' name! Holy Spirit, be my guide to attend to what is revealed to me in Jesus' name that I may survive this sift and excel in the life ordained for me. In Jesus' matchless name I pray, Amen.

Chapter 4

Battle Support

"People lose their way without wise leadership, but a nation succeeds and stands in victory when it has many good counselors to guide it."
– Proverbs 11:14 (TPT)

Just as time is a powerful weapon in the enemy's arsenal, so is isolation. When you are experiencing the onslaught of a sift, you will be seduced with thoughts that are contrary to the Word of God. Yet, those thoughts will often be very close to God's Word. Why is that? Because the enemy knows he must trick you with something that sounds like the truth for you to believe it.

If you think about anything long enough, or recite the same story long enough, it will become a part of your memories as though it actually happened. If the enemy can convince you to isolate during the sift, he knows you'll believe the lies because there is no one to tell you what you are saying or thinking is a gigantic lie. Therefore, a key element to surviving the sift, is support.

Assemble the Troops

Years ago, the Lord taught me a lesson via the National Geographic channel. It's important to note I am not the type of person who sits around watching television shows about nature. I can't tell you how I ended up watching this particular show, but I can tell you it changed my perspective on community.

During the show, the narrator was explaining the famine that was forcing the pride of lion to hunt in areas they typically would have avoided. Because of the migration of the pride, the hyenas in the area were starting to starve because the pride would take any food they killed. After studying the animals for a while, the cameraman caught a lioness that stumbled away from the pride. The hyenas who typically hide from the pride watched to ensure there were no other lions around. When they were sure the coast was clear, they pounced on the lioness and ripped her to shreds. Instantly Holy Spirit whispered to me, "That's what the enemy does when you isolate yourself. He knows he can't defeat you when you are strengthened by your community, but he will attack you when he thinks you are lonely and weak."

To survive the sift, it is important to thwart the enemy's plan by coming out of isolation and sharing what you are experiencing and thinking with others. You need a team of people who can pray with and for you during this process. A proper battle support team requires you to reach up, reach out, and reach down. Let's explore each group of people.

Reach Up

When you reach up, you are reaching for those who are in positions of leadership and authority over you. This could be your pastors or, in some cases, your parents, but it should be people who are stronger and more experienced in their walk with Jesus. You need individuals who have experienced the battle you are walking through. They should have wisdom flowing out of them that gives you strength and strategy.

During the most recent sift I experienced, I felt utterly hopeless. I'd prayed every prayer I knew to pray, fasted, recited every scripture I thought of, and tried every natural remedy. Nothing seemed to work. Then, Holy Spirit told me to reach out to two women and tell them what was going on; my spiritual mom and a spiritual mentor who has walked a very similar path. I reached out to both women within days of each other. Both women gave me wisdom and reminded me of God's Word. They prayed with and for me and gave me strategies to see the promises of God. I saw results immediately and within 2 weeks, the situation was totally resolved in my favor!

Even more than the end result, I felt strengthened when these women poured into me. They joined their faith with mine and knowing I wasn't fighting alone made the load much lighter to bear. I can't stress enough the importance of having people to reach up to! When we humble ourselves enough to ask for help, we are killing pride and the fleshly desire to hide in shame. Every Christian will experience a season of sifting! Instead of being ashamed, we should approach the situation, knowing God trusted us enough to test us. That's a cause for celebration, not a cause for shame!

"And if anyone longs to be wise, ask God for wisdom and he will give it! He won't see your lack of wisdom as an opportunity to scold you over your failures but he will overwhelm your failures with his generous grace." **– James 1:5 (TPT)**

The enemy wants to make you feel ashamed, so you isolate and refuse to reach up. The truth is, there is a Heavenly wisdom for your situation. When you ask God, "How am I going to survive this?" He will often respond through someone He has already placed in your life, a wisdom source He can send your answers through. We often believe God will speak directly to us through His Holy Spirit. And often this is true. However, when you are facing an attack, you've never seen before, you need the gift of wisdom from someone who is more mature in Christ in the area you are fighting. Humbly asking for and receiving this wisdom is vital and can often shorten the length of your sifting process.

Reach Out

When you reach out, you call on your peers, your sisters and brothers in Christ who are on your level. Now, reaching out can be tricky because it may feel as though you are talking to people who can't help because they haven't walked through what you are walking through. This may not necessarily be true.

Because the enemy pushes isolation and shame to keep us from being honest and transparent about what we are facing, you and your sisters and brothers may be experiencing a season of sifting at the same time. This is especially true if you are a member of the same local church. When the enemy is attacking pastors, he also attacks those they serve. His method of operation is to attack leaders from every angle, so if your pastors are in a season of sifting preparing them for promotion, many members of their church will experience a similar attack. If he can remove the support of the pastors, he thinks he can cause them to quit.

When sisters and brothers in Christ expose the plot of the enemy and band together in prayer, Heaven moves to come to their aid. The Bible says where two or three are gathered together in His name; He is in the midst. (Matthew 18:20) When you reach out for help, you become strengthened by the presence of God in your situation AND the knowledge that you are no longer fighting alone. Your sisters and brothers are raising their shields and swords with you in battle. One can chase a thousand, but two will put ten thousand to flight. (Deuteronomy 32:30) This is the prayer of agreement which is far more potent than praying alone.

In my situation, the same week I reached up, I reached out. I called upon the sisters in Christ I trust and asked them to pray with me. As I mentioned earlier, what I had been stumbling through with little results broke within two weeks. But here's the thing: I started to see signs of the battle turning in my favor the same week I asked for help. Why? Because I was no longer fighting alone. My sisters and I were battling shield to shield, and we cut the head of the enemy off in the spirit realm!

Reach Down

Reaching down may be one of the more difficult conversations because it involves asking for support and prayer from those who have either learned from you or those you are in positions of authority over. Human nature is to protect those we cover. However, Kingdom relationships are intended to be reciprocal. That means the people you pour into will one day need to pour back into you.

A great example of this in the Bible is the relationship between Ruth and Naomi. You can find their story in the book of Ruth, chapters one and two. Naomi was Ruth's mother-in-law who, after an extreme season of loss, fell into deep despair. Naomi

65

didn't reach down to Ruth for help, but Ruth refused to allow the elder woman to suffer alone, so she cleaved unto her. Ruth loved Naomi and stuck by her side until an opportunity came for Naomi to feel useful again presented itself.

The Bible does not tell us how long the period of Naomi's despair lasted, but I can imagine there were times when Ruth had to encourage the elder woman. Because Naomi was her mother-in-law, there was a natural order to their relationship. However, when Ruth refused to leave Naomi, we see there was also a covenant relationship at play. There was a great level of respect in Ruth's heart for Naomi. That respect caused Ruth to sympathize with Naomi's sadness instead of judging her for it. When you can see the human brokenness of the one who has poured into you, the correct

Otescia R. Johnson

response is to love and support them until they are able to see clearly again.

> **Instead of acting like Naomi and pushing your people away, reach down to them and ask for their prayers.**

You don't have to give them details they cannot handle, but you need their prayers to help you survive this sift. Remember, the sift is not just a singular attack, this is blow after blow after blow that feels as though the wind is being knocked out of you! You can't afford to be proud and attempt to fight this battle alone. You MUST assemble the troops! Reach up, reach out, and reach down!

Chapter 5

Battle Strategy

Now that your eyes have been opened to see, and you have assembled your troops, it's time to develop your battle strategy. God revealed to me a seven-tactic battle strategy to survive any sift the enemy will ever throw our way. If there is one chapter of this book, you study consistently until it becomes a part of your arsenal; I pray it is this chapter. God would never allow the enemy to sift us without giving us a strategy to overcome! These tactics are shared as God gave them to me, but it is important to note you may shift them around as Holy Spirit leads you.

Otescia R. Johnson

Tactic 1: Prayer

"One day Jesus taught the apostles to keep praying and never stop or lose hope..." – **Luke 18:1 (TPT)**

When you pray, you open the lines of communication with Heaven, which is the starting point for all battles. Prayer is the single most powerful tool of the Believer. Every time you pray, angels are at the ready to carry your petitions to Heaven, and angels are in Heaven ready to deliver God's response. In the 10th chapter of Daniel, God immediately responds to Daniel's prayers, but the kingdom of darkness tries to intercept the angels to delay Daniel's receipt of the answers. A powerful prayer you can release during a sifting is for God to release warring angels to the firmaments to help your messenger angel fight, so your answer can be delivered to you.

Remember, what you are facing is not happenstance. Satan has been slowly and methodically coming up with ways to force you to walk away from what God has promised you. When you pray, be strategic and release the Word of God. Also, a key factor of prayer is to believe God is releasing what you ask for! Belief guarantees your answer!

"Just make sure you ask empowered by confident faith without doubting that you will receive. For the ambivalent person believes one minute and doubts the next. Being undecided makes you become like the rough seas driven and tossed by the wind. You're up one minute and tossed down the next. When you are half-hearted and wavering it leaves you unstable. Can you really expect to receive anything from the Lord when you're in that condition?"

– James 1:6-8 (TPT)

Pray for your battle strategy with full belief that all of Heaven is ready to respond to your request! The strategy has already been prepared because God has already promised you the victory! Ask in faith and receive in faith!

Tactic 2: Praise

"When he had consulted with the people, he appointed those who sang to the Lord and those who praised Him in their holy (priestly) attire, as they went out before the army and said, "Praise and give thanks to the Lord, for His mercy and lovingkindness endure forever. When they began singing and praising, the Lord set ambushes against Judah; so they were struck down [in defeat]." **– 2 Chronicles 20:21-22 (AMP)**

In the scripture referenced above, we find Jehoshaphat in the throes of an attack. The Moabites, Ammonites, and some Meunites

71

band together for this attack. The Bible describes them as a great multitude. Naturally, Jehoshaphat was afraid. In his fear, he did not flee. He employed tactic #1; he prayed. He called for a fast throughout all of Judah.

As we discussed in the last chapter, he reached down for support from the people he led, and they gathered together to seek the Lord. Jehoshaphat was not timid in his request, nor was he prideful in front of the people. Instead, He stood and prayed aloud, reminding God of His sovereignty. He reminded God and all those who were gathered under the sound of his voice of God's track record driving the inhabitants of the land out before Israel and of how God had given the land to the descendants of Abraham.

Then, in the midst of his prayer, Jehoshaphat made a bold statement. He said,

"…we will stand before this house and before You (for Your Name and Your Presence is in this house) and we will cry out to You in our distress, and You will hear and save us."

– 2 Chronicles 20:9 (AMP)

In other words, Jehoshaphat, even though fear attempted to sift him, had faith God would not only hear their prayers, but God would also respond! Prayer plus faith will always equal a response from God.

While they were still assembled, God responded to Jehoshaphat's prayer through Jahaziel. In the response, God not only calmed their fears, but He also assured their victory when He said, *"You need not fight in this battle; take your positions, stand and witness the salvation of the Lord who is with you…"* **– 2 Chronicles 20:17 (AMP**) Hearing God's response, Jehoshaphat bowed in worship.

73

The next morning, when it was time for the battle, Jehoshaphat stood before the people again and gave instructions. Then He appointed the singers and praisers to go out before the army. As they praised, the Lord set an ambush against the enemy. This is the same thing that happens when we praise! The tactic of praise brings confusion to the enemy's camp and causes them to fight amongst themselves! The enemies of Jehoshaphat and Judah destroyed one another until they were all dead. Imagine what is happening in the spirit realm to your enemies when you praise!

Tactic 3: Worship

As we saw in the example with Jehoshaphat, worship is also an essential tactic of war. Worship facilitates intimacy between God and man. It enables us to hear clearly because it helps to silence the world around us so we can hear God's still small voice. I have found that in times of sifting, God does not yell. He whispers so I will have to incline my ear to His lips to hear.

We can find a Biblical reference for this practice in the book of 1 Kings the 19th chapter. Here we find Elijah, who is fresh off his biggest victory to date, yet he is running for his life after Jezebel puts a bounty on his head. As the prophet runs for his life, he finds himself disappointed and alone. It's in that alone time that God begins ministering to him.

During their time alone together, God demonstrates to Elijah that He wasn't in the strong wind, the earthquake, or the fire. Instead, God was in the peaceful, gentle blowing (1 Kings 19:12 NKJV). Elijah immediately recognized God's presence in the small voice and went out to meet Him.

> Had Elijah become distracted by the wind, earthquake, and fire, he would have missed God.

It was in this moment of intimate conversation that Elijah received his instructions. It was the still moment of Elijah's total focus being on God's presence instead of the persecution he was facing or the surrounding noise that led him to the breakthrough he needed. Many of us are guilty of looking for the loud, boisterous move of God in moments that feel critical to our survival, but it's in those moments, God softens His expression to pull us closer to Him. The softer He speaks, the closer we must draw to hear Him. Therefore, worship must always be a part of your battle strategy. We draw nigh to the God of War and He gives us the instructions for victory!

Tactic 4: Cast Down

"Casting down arguments and every high thing that exalts itself against the knowledge of God, bringing every thought into captivity to the obedience of Christ…" **– 2 Corinthians 10:5 (NKJV)**

Remember how we discussed the enemy's tactic of throwing spaghetti at the wall of your mind to see what will stick? Here is the Biblical tactic to stop him in his tracks. The second a thought is suggested that does not line up with the Word of God, you have an instruction to cast it down. This phrase "cast down" means to destroy. How do you destroy a thought? By speaking the Word of God!

It's important to note you cannot defeat a thought with a thought. You must ***speak*** the truth to destroy thoughts. The next part of the scripture refers to a "high thing that exalts itself against the knowledge of God." This is anything that attempts to appear higher than, or more significant than, God and His word. We know God is the only omniscient being. That being said, it is impossible for another being to be more knowledgeable than God in any area! The thought that tries to convince you that you or anyone else knows more than God must be pulled down and destroyed by the Word of God.

It is easy for this type of thought to come and take root in your mind before you know it, because many of us have been receiving and believing these thoughts for as long as we can remember. Here's an example. Let's say you are in prayer one day and you discern by the Holy Spirit that God is calling you to lead in an area of ministry you've never led in before. A thought that is

78

trying to exalt itself against the knowledge of God would say to you, "What do you know about that area? Who are you to lead that? If you were supposed to do that, your pastor would have already asked you to."

Do you see how these thoughts sound like rebuttals we hear and say all the time? That's because the enemy, in his craftiness, has tricked us into believing this is simply asking questions to make sure we heard correctly. He has made these types of thoughts so common; we don't even question their origin. We simply believe they are a part of our mind's way of thinking. When in fact, what we are really doing is allowing a thought to present itself as though it knows more than God.

Still not convinced? Okay, let's examine this further. Imagine you are standing in front of God and He said to you, "I am going to use you to travel around the world and tell people about me. Do not be afraid, for I will be with you wherever you go." Remember, you are standing in front of God. There is no doubt who is talking to you. Do you really think your response would be, "Who am I to travel around the world?" Or would you be more likely to fall at His feet and worship because you are so humbled, honored, and grateful to be chosen for the assignment? For most of us, it would be the latter because there would be no thoughts of doubt as you watch the words leave from God's mouth.

In His presence, you would be sure of your call and assignment. Why is that not true in your everyday life? Because the enemy is constantly throwing thoughts at you that undermine what God has spoken as though the devil, or even you, could possibly know more than God about your purpose here in the earth. If we're not careful to cast the lie down, those types of thoughts take root in us and instead of us depending on and adhering to every word that proceeds out of the mouth of God, we end up challenging Him on everything He says.

If you can master this battle tactic, you can win the war happening in your mind. As soon as the thought comes up, recite a scripture, declaration, or confession that puts you and your thoughts back in your rightful place, with your ear to God's lips in an intimate posture of worship. Once you hear what God has to say, repeat it aloud. Confess it until you believe what you're saying because we know faith comes by hearing and hearing by the word of God. (Romans 10:17 NKJV)

Tactic 5: Repent and Denounce

"Or say you're out on the street and an old enemy accosts you. Don't lose a minute. Make the first move; make things right with him. After all, if you leave the first move to him, knowing his track record, you're likely to end up in court, maybe even jail. If that happens, you won't get out without a stiff fine."
– Matthew 5:25-56 (MSG)

While you are in the middle of a sift, the enemy will attempt to pull you out of your position of victory by reminding you of all the sinful things you've done in your past. You may begin to feel condemnation about things you know you've already repented of and been forgiven for. This is because the enemy wants you to feel as though you are not worthy of receiving the promise on the other side of this sift. He wants thoughts of condemnation to leave you

82

feeling unworthy to reign supreme as lord of your thoughts. However, we can pull on the Word of God to shut him down.

Instead of arguing with the enemy regarding your past, quickly agree and repent. Yes, I did _____ (insert your sin) and I repent and come out of agreement with the kingdom of darkness. I close every demonic door, window, or portal that may have been opened in my life as a result of this sin. I repent on behalf of anyone in my bloodline and denounce any demonic activity they may have been involved in. I come out of agreement with and divorce anything they agreed to that is not like God. I cleanse my entire bloodline with the blood of Jesus and dedicate my life to serving Jesus.

Too often we waste time trying to prove our own innocence when we serve an omniscient God who has never missed a single moment of our lives. He has witnessed it all and has an excellent score card. We do not have to defend ourselves against a liar, when God already knows the truth and Jesus is consistently making intercession for us!

1 John 2:1-2 (NLT) – *"My dear children, I am writing this to you so that you will not sin. But if anyone does sin, we have an advocate who pleads our case before the Father. He is Jesus Christ, the one who is truly righteous. He himself is the sacrifice that atones for our sins — and not only our sins but the sins of the world."*

I can't stress enough the importance of not allowing the enemy to steal your time through his accusations regarding your past. Not only did Jesus atone for it, but He also carries the responsibility of being our advocate. Advocate in this text means one who pleads another's cause with one, an intercessor. Though the enemy is attempting to sift you, please know Jesus is on His job, defending you to God the Father. You do not need to waste time defending yourself or trying to prove how worthy you are. Instead, confess the sin and repent with full assurance that what you have repented for has been forgiven and that Jesus is defending you directly to God. Denounce and renounce any and all things you and your ancestors may have done that gave the enemy access to your life. And finally, move forward in confidence that you are forgiven and free from the demonic stronghold that tried to condemn you and keep you in bondage!

Tactic 6: Affirm and Decree

I've written a book on how to properly write and release affirmations and declarations based on God's word, so I won't spend a ton of time here, but just in case you haven't read that book yet, let's define these two terms.

Affirm- to confirm thoroughly

Decree- utterance; recital, written account

Affirmations are your "I AM" statements that thoroughly confirm what God has already said about you and your purpose. When you issue a decree, you are giving the earth a command it must obey through your utterance, recital, and/or written account of what God has said.

The Bible says in Job 22:28 (NKJV), *"You will also decree a thing, and it will be established for you…"* This means, what you decree with your mouth will be accomplished in the Earth. When you are in the midst of a sifting process, what you speak matters because what you speak reveals what you believe. This is one of the ways the enemy knows whether or not what he is throwing at you is working. Your words reveal your nature and the content of your heart according to the 12th chapter of the book of Matthew.

"...*For out of the abundance of the heart, the mouth speaks.*" – **Matthew 12:34** (NJKV)

What you speak tells the enemy his attack against you is either effective or ineffective! This is why it is imperative your words confirm what God has said. Additionally, if you continue reading in Matthew chapter 12, you'll find verse 37 that says, *"For by your words you will be justified, and by your words you will be condemned."* The word justified in this sense means to be declared righteous! In other words, God is listening to what you are saying in the midst of the sift!

Coming into agreement with what He said rather than the lies the enemy fed you is what will determine your righteousness!

Yes, you will think all sorts of crazy thoughts, BUT what matters most to God is what you say! What comes out of your mouth becomes what you see because the Bible also says, *"Death and life are in the power of the tongue, and those who love it will eat its fruit."* (Proverbs 18:21 NKJV) You possess enough power in your tongue to create the life you want to see AND prove your righteousness!

Therefore, the tactic of affirming and decreeing is a powerful weapon in the arsenal of a Believer. Your words are literally shaping the world around you. When you are in the middle of the test of time, you have the power in your tongue to shift time in your favor. You can call what you need out of Heaven and command it to appear in the earth realm.

Let me give you an example of how I tested this law. In 2016, after having to start our lives over from scratch, my husband and I were facing a major financial crisis. The mortgage was severely behind, and we were in danger of losing our home due to no fault of our own. We'd tried everything we knew to try, and doors were constantly being slammed in our faces. Exhausted from all the financial pressure, I began to pray and cry out to God.

During the prayer, a righteous boldness rose up in me and I demanded our financial season to change. I spoke to the atmosphere and commanded what belonged to us to be released into our hands. I'd never prayed from a position of authority in this manner, but I knew I'd had an encounter with God during the prayer. He was teaching me a new way to access what I needed. Over the next 5 months, I watched God do the impossible. Everything that should have taken us months or years to accomplish happened so fast it felt like we were living in Amos 9:13-15 (MSG)

"Yes indeed, it won't be long now." God's decree. "Things are going to happen so fast your head will swim, one thing fast on the heels of the other. You won't be able to keep up. Everything will be happening at once—and everywhere you look, blessings! Blessings like wine pouring off the mountains and hills. I'll make everything right again for my people Israel: "They'll rebuild their ruined cities. They'll plant vineyards and drink good wine. They'll work their gardens and eat fresh vegetables. And I'll plant them, plant them on their own land. They'll never again be uprooted from the land I've given them." God your God, says so."

Tactic 7: Rest

I have a dear friend, Roshanda Pratt, who lives by the phrase, "rest is a weapon". I've never been a huge fan of sleeping beyond what is absolutely necessary for my body. Even as a kid, I despised naps. But in this most recent sift, I clearly heard the Lord say to me, "Rest is a weapon." When I heard the phrase, I was mentally overwhelmed and exhausted, even though my body did not feel sleepy. Armed with the phrase and the following scripture, I employed the tactic of rest for the first time.

"For God speaks once, And even twice, yet no one notices it [including you, Job]. In a dream, a vision of the night [one may hear God's voice], when deep sleep falls on men While slumbering upon the bed, Then He opens the

ears of men And seals their instruction." –
Job 33:14-16 (AMP)

In the heat of a sift, it can be very difficult to silence your emotions enough to hear God's instruction. If you are anything like me, you like to find solutions to problems rather than wait for a solution to fall into your lap. While this may work for you in other seasons of your life, during a sift, your responsibility is to maintain your faith, meaning things are going to look very bleak during the threshing and winnowing and you won't be able to do anything about it. In seasons like this, you are literally waiting upon God for solutions, deliverance, healing, provision, and ultimately, promotion.

To keep you from getting in your own way and making your situation worse, God will often block things that may have worked for you in the past. This can lead to great frustration. In the moments of frustration and feeling hopeless, rest is your greatest weapon. You can lie down and ask God to speak to you as you sleep.

While in the sifting, I employed this strategy three separate times. Each time, I silently asked God to give me peace, physical and mental restoration, and direction while I slept. The first occasion was the day I described earlier in this book. It was the day I cried in the car as the devil tried to seduce me into giving up. When we returned home that day, I was mentally drained, so I took a nap and woke up an hour later with the song "*I Almost Let Go*" by Kurt Carr in my spirit.

Now, for reference's sake, I want to add I had not heard that song for many years. In fact, it has been so long that I initially could not remember the name of the artist. I just kept hearing the chorus echo in my spirit over and over until I sang the song aloud. The words below are not in the correct order of the song, but this is how they came to me at that moment, so I'm quoting them not as they are written and performed, but as God allowed me to remember them so my spirit could be encouraged.

"I almost let go. I was right at the edge of a breakthrough and couldn't see it. The devil thought he had me, but Jesus came and grabbed me, and God held me close, so I wouldn't let go."

Again, this is not how the song goes, but I was receiving the words in the order I needed to hear them for my specific situation. I remember waking up from that nap so encouraged that God heard my silent plea for help as I closed my eyes and answered me! I went into my bathroom and cried and worshipped God from the depths of my being. Immediately, I was 100% sure all things would work out in my favor.

The second time I employed this strategy was four days later. During those four days, my husband and I were hit with multiple blows of bad news. Saturday's confidence was wearing thin. After a particularly disappointing phone call, I cried out to God, "What are we supposed to do? I've tried everything I know to do, and nothing is working! Everyone is counting on us. Please, just tell us what to do." Again, I heard the phrase, rest is a weapon, so I took another nap.

This time I had a dream about a benefactor coming into our lives and signing paperwork for us. Then, as I woke up, I heard, *"After you've done all you can, you just stand."* It's a line from the song *"Stand"* by

95

Donnie McClurkin. Again, this song was released in 1996 and I can't remember the last
time I listened to it or even heard anyone
mention it. It was clear to me God was using songs to encourage me and give me answers during this sift. To my recollection,
God has never spoken to me in this manner,
but I've also never intentionally employed
rest as a battle tactic.

      Finally, three days later (exactly one
week after I silently cried in the car) we received what seemed to be our first sign of
good news. I felt like the tide was beginning
to turn in our favor. I went to sleep that
night and woke up hearing, *"It's over now. It's
over now. I feel like I can make it. The storm is over
now."* This time, I had no idea who wrote the
song or the title of it, because I don't think
I've heard it since the 90s. Thank God for
YouTube because I was able to quickly

locate the song by Kirk Franklin and God's Property.

Again, I worshipped God and cried tears of relief as I was 100% certain I'd finally survived the sift and a remedy to our problem was soon to come! I can't tell you the weight that lifted off my shoulders as I sang those song lyrics over and over. The intensity of the battle was short-lived, but the truth is, God was telling me that my family and I were ending one era and walking into another. It was bigger than the problem that was immediately in our faces. The "kitchen sink" attack was the end of a multi-year test and we'd finally passed! We survived the sift!

Chapter 6

Walk Light

> *"And Elijah said to them, "Seize the prophets of Baal! Do not let one of them escape!" So they seized them; and Elijah brought them down to the Brook Kishon and executed them there. Then Elijah said to Ahab, "Go up, eat and drink; for there is the sound of abundance of rain."* **– 1 Kings 18:40-41 (NKJV)**

The most dangerous moment in the life of a Believer is the moment after a victory. In the scripture above, the Prophet Elijah was in between two victories. The first victory was when he alone defeated 450 prophets of Baal. Immediately afterwards, he released word that the drought was about to end. If you read 1

Kings chapters 18 and 19, you'll see Elijah was a prophet among prophets because while others hid in caves out of fear for their lives, he listened to the guidance of the Lord and had a showdown in front of all the children of Israel.

His victory in front of the people caused Israel to turn back to God, but it also put him in Jezebel's cross hairs. So, after the victory and the abundance of rain that ended the drought, Elijah found himself running for his life, all alone, and full of despair. In that moment, one would think it should be a time of rejoicing, but Elijah was praying for death.

"...It is enough! Now Lord, take my life, for I am not better than my fathers!" **– 1 Kings 19:4 (NKJV)**

I would imagine Elijah's prayer resulted from wondering what was the point of the great display of the power of God on

Mount Carmel, if he was still going to end up alone and afraid for his life like all the other prophets. Where do you think Elijah got those thoughts? You guessed it! This is a perfect example of how we feel when the enemy's spaghetti sticks to the walls of our minds!

Most people rush right to rejoicing after a victory, but after a sift there is a short window of time known as ascension. Remember, the purpose of the sift is to test your faith and prepare you for promotion. Before you can experience the promotion in the spirit, you must ascend to a higher elevation. The hour of ascension is short, but can often be turbulent.

Think of how you feel when an airplane is taking off. Though the plane is well equipped and able to combat the wind and atmospheric changes, it experiences as it elevates to higher heights, passengers inside the plane can still feel the resistance of the

100

air as it ascends. The same is true in the spirit. Though you have survived the sift, the enemy is waiting for the opportunity to attack you again as you ascend. This is why walking light is important.

If you are not familiar with the phrase "walk light", it is used to encourage as little unnecessary chatter, activity, or engagement as possible. We typically employ this strategy after major ministry events, life changes, and battles. Think of a new mother after she has just given birth. She is encouraged to move as she needs to, but not overdo it to ensure her body heals correctly. Walking light means to do what you must and only what you must.

After a sift, you will experience a moment of ascension related resistance. This can look like money being held up, a senseless argument with a friend or family member, news that seems bad, or someone initially saying no before coming back to you with a yes. The "turbulence" you experience in this moment is the enemy's attempt to steal your focus away from what God has prepared you to receive. Your job during ascension is to trust the pilot, God.

If you walk light during the moment of ascension and remained focused on the promised promotion, you will see God's promise revealed in ways you never imagined. Going back to our example in the book of Kings, Elijah experienced the turbulence and had a momentary mental setback before God gave him instructions for his next level of ministry.

"Then the Lord said to him: "Go, return on your way to the Wilderness of Damascus; and when you arrive, anoint Hazael as king over Syria. Also you shall anoint Jehu the son of Nimshi as king over Israel. And Elisha the son of Shaphat of Abel Meholah you shall anoint as prophet in your place." – **1 Kings 19:15-16 (NKJV)**

At first glance, one reading this may think, wait, God's reward to Elijah is to replace him? The answer is yes. When you are promoted by God, someone else must also be trained and promoted to take your place. Since Elijah had literally just finished complaining to God about the bounty on his head, one would think God would address his concerns and comfort his fears. Instead, God resisted speaking to what had already been settled. Elijah had already survived the sift! He was in the middle of an ascension.

> There was no need to rehash what had already been defeated.

When Elijah immediately followed God's instructions, his actions were decreeing, "I trust God and I accept my promotion!" This act of obedience caused him to walk right into his promotion as he met Elisha, the one who would sit at his feet, serve him, and receive a double portion of his anointing when Elijah's assignment in the earth was complete. In 2 Kings chapter 2, when Elijah was taken into Heaven by a whirlwind, Elisha was there, ready to receive the mantle Elijah left behind. Elijah's faithfulness to God, and his ability to walk light after victory, empowered him to complete his assignment, cheat death, and have enough power to empower Elisha!

Though Elijah's humanity was on display during his moment of ascension, we still see the hand of God upon him, and God's promises revealed. Elijah's journey into the wilderness away from people was initiated by Jezebel's threat to kill him but remember God causes all things to work together for our good! (Romans 8:28)

What looked like running away was actually Elijah walking light. How can I say that? Well, in the wilderness, Elijah only did what was absolutely necessary. He wasn't releasing any miracles, having showdowns with false prophets, or releasing the word of the Lord to anyone. He was only doing what he absolutely had to do each day. He was still while the pilot (God) pushed through the turbulence of his thinking and guided him to spiritual promotion!

> When you learn to walk light you minimize the opportunities the enemy has to steal, kill, and destroy.

Just as rest is a weapon, remaining vigilant and aware of the enemy's devices keeps his weapons from prospering. In the season of ascension, refrain from making new plans or launching into new projects. The last thing you want to do is give the enemy something new to attach to as you ascend to your next level. Instead, spend quality time with the Father, with your ear inclined to His lips. Seek His face and not His hand. Worship Him for who He is without asking Him, what is to come. There will be time after your ascension to the next level to ask for instructions. For now, trust God, and move only when necessary.

Chapter 7

Collect Your Spoils

Immediately following the sift and ascension, it is time to collect the spoils of war. If all things really work together for your good, you will see a downpour of spiritual and natural blessings after you survive the sift.

"When Jehoshaphat and his people came to take away their spoil, they found among them an abundance of valuables on the dead bodies, and precious jewelry, which they stripped off for themselves, more than they could carry away; and they were three days gathering the spoil

because there was so much." **– 2 Chronicles 20:25 (NKJV)**

In the example above, Jehoshaphat and his army watched as God kept His promise of victory to them. As it was customary in their day for the victor to collect the spoils of war, they walked amongst the dead bodies of their enemies and took what now belonged to them. Their enemies had so many valuables on their physical bodies it took Jehoshaphat and his men 3 days to collect it all. God's reward for their victory in battle was to transfer the wealth of their enemy into their hands.

Going back to our foundational scripture for this book, what if the reason God gave the enemy permission to sift you was because He wanted to transfer the wealth of the kingdom of darkness into your hands? The Bible says in Proverbs

13:22 (NKJV), *"...But the wealth of the sinner is stored up for the righteous."* After you are promoted, God causes what has been "stored up" to be released to you as spoils. This ensures we remember what God delivered us from, as well as what He prepared for us as our reward for steadfast endurance during the battle.

God has to make the spoils of war far outweigh the difficulty of the sift. Otherwise, it would look as though the impact of the enemy is greater than the VICTORY of God. This is why we often see people pop on the scene as what appears to be an overnight success. The individuals start to see massive success and expansion in their lives, which causes onlookers to wonder where they came from. Spiritually speaking, they just survived a sift!

You see, in a sift, you may appear to be a well-kept secret because God is removing everyone and everything that can't participate in the collection of your spoils. You may feel as though you are losing everything but in actuality God is blowing away the chaff, the useless things that served you in your last season but cannot serve you in the next. After you survive the sift, you walk in expansion, advancement, and acceleration in the area you were just sifted in!

This is why we can rejoice during and after a sift. The enemy thought the sift would be your end and, in a sense, he was correct. The sift is the end of stagnation and cycles of delay, but more importantly, it is the beginning of your manifested promise!

> Do not let old religious mindsets stop you from collecting your spoils.

You did not survive what you just survived just so you can go back to business as usual! You survived to thrive! I know it sounds like a cliché, but it is true! God allowed the sifting for your benefit. When you survive the sift, turn your attention to the reward! This season didn't just happen *to* you, it happened **FOR YOU**! Go collect your spoils!

Chapter 8

Si Vis Pacem, Para Bellum

Pray for Peace, Prepare for War

Years ago, while living in Germany, my husband and I had the pleasure of serving under the leadership of Pastor James Fleming. Pastor Fleming is unlike any other person I've ever met. He had several sayings that I'm sure will remain with me as long as I'm alive. "We pray for peace, but we prepare for war" is one of those sayings. He'd often use this phrase to remind us that even though our request is to see peace, we must remember we are always in the midst of a spiritual battle.

When Holy Spirit prompted me to end this book with this chapter, I did an internet search of the phrase to see where it originated. I was surprised to learn it is from the Latin phrase: "Si Vis Pacem, Para Bellum", which when translated into English means "If You Want Peace, Prepare For War." It was derived from a much older phrase written by a Roman author in the fourth or fifth century AD. This means the cycles of war and peace are not new, meaning the enemy has had centuries to perfect his craft. You and I are the ones who are new to the party. But thank God, we have access to the playbook and strategies to win every battle launched against us! The key is recognizing winning one battle does not mean you've won the war.

Yes, you've survived THIS sift, but just as sure as you are reading this book right now, Satan will once again ask for permission to sift you. He will take his time to prepare another "kitchen sink attack" when you least expect it. Right before the next major elevation and expansion in your life, he will approach God and ask for permission to turn your life upside down.

> The key to continuously surviving the sift is to acknowledge this is a cycle!

Times of war are followed by times of peace. Times of peace are followed by times of war. The only way you lose in times of war is if you refuse to prepare in times of peace. After every major battle, look to God for guidance and direction. We've already discussed the importance of walking light, but it's deeper than that. During times of peace, you must add to your spiritual arsenal so that your weapons and your ability to use them both remain sharp.

One way I've learned to remain sharp is by asking God to direct me to sermons and other Biblical teachings that will support me in my current season and the one to come. Spending time in the Word of God is one of our greatest weapons because it holds the keys to overcoming Satan and our fleshly nature.

Using the Word to Defeat Satan

In the 4th chapter of the book of Matthew, after Jesus fasted forty days and forty nights, the tempter (Satan) came to him. Now, Jesus had been led by the Spirit into the wilderness to be tempted. This means the encounter He had with the devil was not by chance or happenstance. It was designed by God.

During this moment when Jesus was physically hungry, the enemy offers Him food, and Jesus replies only with the

115

Word of God. *"It is written, Man shall not live by bread alone, but by every word that proceeds from the mouth of God."* **– Matthew 4:4** (NKJV) We know Jesus was fully man and fully God while He walked the Earth, but His physical body required food just like yours and mine. It would have been easy for Him to give in and accept the food, but Jesus understood this was a critical time for Him. Satan tried to exploit Jesus' human vulnerabilities, hoping to tempt Him into misusing His God-nature in a manner that went against God's will at that time.

Instead of Jesus listening to the demands of His physical body or entertaining unnecessary conversation with the enemy, He simply rebuked Satan with the Word. This simple act of responding with the Word kept Jesus in right standing with God and shut the enemy down. Next, Satan attempted to lure Jesus by taking Him up into the holy city and setting Him on a pinnacle. He tempted Jesus by telling him to throw Himself down and then quoted scripture to make his point.

> "...If You are the son of God, throw Yourself down. For it is written: 'He shall give His angels charge over you,' and 'In their hands they shall bear you up, lest you dash your foot against a stone.'"– **Matthew 4:6 (NKJV)**

In this second attempt, Satan makes a mockery of Jesus' quotation of scripture by quoting his own. Now we know and understand this was an accurate scripture but also a blatant misuse of it. Because Jesus was not ignorant of the devices of Satan, He once again stood His ground and let the Word of God do the heavy lifting.

Finally, Satan tried a third time to tempt Jesus. This time, he tried to offer

Jesus all the kingdoms of the world and their glory in exchange for Jesus' worship. This time, Jesus not only rebuked Satan with the Word of God, but He also commanded Satan to leave!

> *"Then the devil left Him and behold, angels came and ministered to Him."* **– Matthew 4:11 (NKJV)**

It's important to note Jesus endured the enemy for a time because He understood the tempting was necessary. However, once the enemy asked Jesus to bow and worship him, Jesus exercised His kingdom authority and commanded the devil to leave. In this scripture, Jesus gives us a clear picture of **James 4:7 (NKJV)** *"Therefore submit to God. Resist the devil and He will flee from you."*

Jesus' submission came by way of Him following the leading of the Spirit into the wilderness. His resistance to the devil came by way of Him standing firm in His faith and using the word of God to defeat Satan. This is the example of how we should all respond to the tempting of the devil.

Satan could have come to tempt Jesus at any moment, but he came when he knew Jesus would be physically weak. This was an attempt to sift Jesus and test His faith! This is how Jesus could speak to Peter with such certainty. He'd already experienced the attempted sifting personally!

What does this have to do with praying for peace and preparing for war?

Jesus spent 40 days and 40 nights fasting and praying. During that intimate time alone in the wilderness with the Father, I can only imagine the communion Jesus was experiencing. If you've ever undergone an extended fast, you know the presence of

God will linger with you during that time. Imagine how amazing it must have been for Jesus, who was the son of God. That is the purest definition of peace I can imagine.

Yet, before Jesus could even be physically restored and after His spirit had been greatly charged in the presence of God, there was the devil. Because He prepared during His time of peace, which was His time in the presence of God, Jesus was ready for war! He was empowered with the Word to rebuke the devil at every turn. Nothing the devil said worked because Jesus was armed with the Word that is sharper than any two-edged sword!

If you continue reading in Matthew chapter 4, you'll see that Jesus had a brief moment of ascension. This was when the angels came and ministered to Him. This was his moment of walking light. But immediately following that moment, Jesus' Galilean ministry began, meaning He walked into promotion!

His ministry and all the lives that would be transformed through their encounters with Him depended upon Jesus, not only surviving the sift, but preparing for war. Satan did not catch Jesus by surprise, because Jesus was prepared. He was armed with the Word! He was committed to the will of His Father in Heaven. And because of His commitment and preparation, a time of promotion immediately followed His time of sifting!

If you are hungry, angry, lonely, or tired… **HALT!** Slow down and think before you act or speak. These are key moments the enemy will attempt to attack you. These attacks are similar to the way Jesus was tempted in the wilderness, which means

121

you have the strategy to defeat them with the Word of God. If you make preparation a part of your lifestyle, these attacks will not find you without a sharpened weapon!

> *"For the word of God is living and powerful, and sharper than any two-edged sword, piercing even to the division of the soul and spirit, and the joints and marrow, and is a discerner of the thoughts and intents of the heart."* — **Hebrews 4:12 (NKJV)**

Using the Word to Overcome Fleshly Temptation

Sometimes the attacks do not come directly from the enemy. They come from the heat and desires of your own flesh. This is especially true if you allow your mind to become idle during times of peace. Again, consistently feeding yourself with the word of God and developing a daily discipline of spending time in His presence will help to keep you sharp spiritually. Yet, you are human and wrapped in flesh, therefore there will be moments you will be tempted to listen to the desires of your flesh.

The desires of the flesh can come in many forms, but they always entail doing what feels good in the moment versus what is eternally good. *"For all that is in the world— the lust of the flesh, the lust of the eyes, and the pride of life—is not of the Father but is of the world. And the world is passing away, and the lust of it; but he who does the will of God abides forever." –* **1 John 2:16-17 (NKJV)** The things that please the flesh will always relate to the human experience. It can range from things like engaging in sexual activity outside the covenant of marriage to gossiping about someone. All of it is rooted in the temporal experience and lacks the ability to bring Glory to God.

I often tell the story of how I was once really upset over the fact that a piece of furniture I ordered from a furniture store had been sold to another customer. I'd searched for this furniture for six months before ordering it and waited for weeks for it to arrive, only to be told someone else was allowed to buy what I'd already paid for. The salesperson was very apologetic, but my flesh felt justifiably angry. I didn't want a replacement or a refund! I wanted the furniture I'd been waiting for weeks to receive.

During my encounter with the salesperson, I kept hearing the phrase, "Don't ruin your witness" in my spirit. It wasn't easy, but I was able to keep my cool and keep my flesh under subjection. A few weeks later, I was ministering during an event at church and who walks in the door? The salesperson! I was so grateful I'd listened to my spirit instead of my flesh because had I responded in anger and said harsh things to the salesperson, she would not have been able to receive the word of God from me.

How did I do it? How did I overcome my flesh at that moment? Because I had a lifestyle of studying the Word of God and spending time with Him daily, my spirit was stronger than my flesh. I practiced killing my flesh daily by starving it as much as possible. When you live a lifestyle of feeding your spirit and starving your flesh, it is easier to hear when Holy Spirit is speaking to you. Your flesh is less likely to rise when it has been weakened by starvation.

Praying for peace while we prepare for war should be the lifestyle of all Believers. As long as we live, there will be cycles of war and peace. This should never catch us by surprise. The key to success will always be our dedication and attention to the things of God. Surviving the Sift is not a one-time occurrence. This is a way of life for those of us who are growing in and with God! As long as you walk with God, you'll be given opportunity after opportunity to survive the sift. Starve your flesh, feed your spirit, and remain aware of your assured victory in Christ! This sift was not happenstance, it was orchestrated for your promotion! Keep your eyes on the prize. You can do this, my friend. I believe in you!

About the Author

Otescia R. Johnson is a skilled writer, captivating and innovative speaker, bestselling author, publisher, mindset coach, and minister of the Gospel. She holds a Bachelor of Science degree in Business Administration and has dedicated her life to helping Kingdom Entrepreneurs walk out their assignment in marketplace ministry.

In 2012, Otescia founded O. Johnson Ministries, an effort aimed at equipping the whole woman to walk in the fullness of her purpose! She then launched the "Healing the Hurt" conference, which speaks to the broken places women often try to hide. In addition to managing O. Johnson Ministries, Otescia is the founder of B.O.Y. (Bet on Yourself) Enterprises, Inc., a corporation that helps believers merge their faith and business as they navigate the world of entrepreneurship. She is also the bestselling author of 17 published books, journals, and planners, as well as the creator of the *Magnetize Your Life* and *Roadmap to Publication* systems.

Otescia is a firm believer in the sanctity of marriage and enjoys being married to her best friend and biggest supporter, Lyndell Johnson. They have devoted their lives to each other, their children, and their grandchildren. They currently reside in North Carolina.

To connect with Otescia or to invite her to speak at your event, visit her website:

www.otesciajohnson.com

Other books by Otescia R. Johnson

Goodbye Egypt- A Kingdom Entrepreneur's Guide to Reclaiming the Marketplace

God Says I Am- A Guide to Fruitful Affirmations and Declarations

I Am Who I Am... and I'm Finally Cool with Her

He Cheated- A Woman's Guide to Receiving God's Healing After Adultery

Hello reader,

Did you enjoy *Surviving the Sift?* If so, please go to Amazon and leave an honest review. Reviews play a pivotal role in the success of any publication, but this is especially true for independently published books such as this one. Please scan the QR Code below to be directed to Amazon to leave a review to ensure more readers know how powerful and impactful this book is.

Thanks in advance,

Otescia